LEGENDS OF THE PEAK

Louise Maskill

BRADWELL
BOOKS

Published by Bradwell Books
Carrwood Road, Chesterfield S41 9QB
Email: info@bradwellbooks.co.uk

All rights reserved. No part of this publication may be reproduced, stored in a retrieval system or transmitted in any form or by any means, electronic, mechanical, photocopying, recording or otherwise without the prior permission of Bradwell Books.

British Library Cataloguing in Publication Data: a catalogue record for this book is available from the British Library.

1st Edition

ISBN: 9781912060702

Design by: Andrew Caffrey

Typesetting by: Mark Titterton

Photograph Credits: iStock, Mark Titterton and credited individually.
Front Cover: Castleton Garland Day - Mark Titterton

Print: CPI Group (UK) Ltd, Croydon, CR0 4YY

CONTENTS

Introduction	4
Heroes and Villains	6
Witches and the Devil	14
Black Dogs, Rams and Other Strange Beasts	24
Hauntings and Curses	29
Hobs, Giants, Fairies and Other Spirits of Place	36
Pools, Rivers and Other Water Sources	44
Superstitions and Omens	51
Good Luck, Bad Luck	54
The Journey Through Life	57
The Wheel of the Year	64
A Peak District Miscellany	76

INTRODUCTION

The folk tales and folklore of the British Isles make for an endlessly fascinating study. The cultural melting pot of ancient Britain has bequeathed us an eclectic mix of heroes, villains, myths and legends, and over the centuries a glorious confusion of beliefs has evolved to account for phenomena both natural and supernatural, and to explain, inhabit and name landscape features such as hills, rivers, woods, chasms, moors and marshes.

Our ancestors lived very different lives to those we enjoy today. Most were tied to the land and had intimate relationships with the changing seasons and the natural world. Few travelled further than their local environs and perhaps the nearest market town, but this seemingly limited existence was nevertheless richly coloured

with an awareness of another world, where supernatural beings existed just outside mortal awareness, where illness and death could be caused not by germs or viruses but by witchcraft, and where mythical heroes could be brought to life in dramatic stories and legends retold down the generations.

In this book you will be introduced to some of the legends and folklore which enriched the days and nights of the folk of the Peak District and its surrounding environs. You will meet fairies, hobs, witches, giants and the Devil, and you will encounter heroic legendary figures such as Robin Hood, Llywarch the bard and a pair of battling kings from the Dark Ages. You will read about murders, highwaymen, curses, superstitions and omens for both good and bad luck, the ceremonies and rituals associated with the rural year and critical stages in life, and learn about a few particularly Peak District customs and traditions.

Welcome to the Peak District, a truly magical part of the world!

HEROES AND VILLAINS

Like other areas of the Midlands and northern England, the Peak District has many associations with the archetypal English folk hero Robin Hood. Many landscape features are named after him – rock formations, caves, valleys, streams, rivers and wells – and most have stories connected to them.

The famous outlaw and his band are said to have spent time in Longdendale in the northwest of Derbyshire when the Sheriff of Nottingham made Sherwood Forest too hot for them. Robin Hood's Picking Rods, a pair of stone columns set into a stone base near the village of Charlesworth, were once shot at by the outlaw during an archery competition to win the freedom of a fair maiden. His arrow is said to have left the groove in one of the columns which can still be seen today.

The well-known Robin Hood's Cave on Stanage Edge, where the outlaw is thought to have lived for a while, lies near to the reputed birthplace of Robin's faithful lieutenant Little John in Hathersage. Before he joined the outlaws John followed the traditional craft of nailor, and after many years and adventures in and around Sherwood Forest he returned to his birthplace after Robin's death. His grave is in Hathersage churchyard; it is some ten feet long, and when it was excavated an unusually large and strong thigh bone was found. At his burial his last arrow was driven into the ground near his grave, and it sprouted and grew into a tree to shade his final resting place. His cap and longbow once hung in Hathersage church, although they were later removed for safekeeping.

The gravestone of Little John, in the churchyard of the Church of St Michael in Hathersage.
CC Paul Walker

Travelling the roads and trackways of rural England was once much more perilous than it is today. In the aftermath of the English Civil War many ex-soldiers, perhaps having found themselves on the losing side and therefore penniless, took to the roads and became highwaymen, robbing unwary travellers and turning some isolated areas into bandit country, to be traversed only in numbers and with armed protection. Even this was often not enough, however; one highway robber remembered in Derbyshire is Black Harry, who plied his trade on the turnpike roads around Wardlow. He had a busy and successful career – until he was caught, convicted and hanged in Gibbet Field near Wardlow. He is still remembered in local place names such as Black Harry Gate, Black Harry Lane and the former Black Harry Farm.

There are two hills north of village of Hope, separated by the River Noe; they are known as Win Hill and Lose Hill, and a rather fanciful local legend connects them with a great battle which is said to have taken place around and between them in the seventh century. The battle was between Edwin, King of Northumbria, and Cruichelm, one of the kings of Wessex; at that time this part of the Peaks lay on the ancient border between Northumbria and Mercia, and Cruichelm was allied with the Mercians to oppose Edwin's expansionist ambitions.

Edwin's and Cruichelm's armies occupied the two heights and battle was joined across the lower land between them. The River Noe is said to have run red with blood, but eventually Edwin's forces, camped on what would become Win Hill, prevailed by rolling huge boulders down the hillside against the attacking Wessex army. The two hills were named Win and Lose in memory of the fates of Edwin's and Cruichelm's armies, while the stones were later collected and turned into millstones, now the symbol of the Peak District National Park.

Unfortunately there is little historical evidence for this tale; it is more likely that the hills' names come from the Anglo-Saxon words for willow (*wythine*) and pigsties (*hlose*). Likewise, the connection with millstones relates more to their historic production in the area's gritstone quarries as far back as the thirteenth century. Nevertheless, this is a stunning landscape and it is certainly easy to imagine the battlecries of our ancestors echoing from the hilltops.

In Back Forest, above Gradbach between Leek and Buxton, is one of the most dramatic and beautiful locations in the Staffordshire moorlands. Lud's Church is a chasm one hundred metres long and eighteen metres deep, caused by a massive land slip in the distant past and now known for its history, mystery and natural beauty.

Win Hill, from Bamford Edge.
iStock

The path that winds along the chasm floor is cool and damp, and the vegetation is mossy and overgrown; Lud's Church has an atmosphere all its own, which has attracted lovers, conspirators and outlaws down the centuries (as well as television crews!).

Its name is reputed to come from Walter de Ludank or de Lud-Auk, a local man from the early fifteenth century. Walter was a Lollard, the name given to a religious sect who were followers of John Wycliffe. Lollard religious observance was banned largely because it rejected the acquisition of wealth by the church, and Lud's Church was used by members of the sect as a secret place of worship. However, on at least one occasion they were discovered and Walter de Ludank was arrested, giving his name to the place of his downfall. Another connection with the Lollards may be the wooden ship's figurehead who used to stand in a rocky niche above the path. Known as Lady Lud, she was thought to commemorate the death of the daughter of a Lollard preacher.

However, as with all good stories there are alternative versions; some contend that the name comes from a horse named Lud, who was carrying a huntsman in pursuit of a deer through the dense forest above. The huntsman did not notice the chasm gaping before him, but Lud did; he skidded to a halt, bucked and threw his rider to his death on the rocky chasm floor. The huntsman is reputed to still wander the area, green, mossy and overgrown and perhaps still searching for his deer (or his horse).

Local legend also connects the chasm with Robin Hood, Friar Tuck and Bonnie Prince Charlie, all of whom are said to have hidden here, and it is also thought to be the location of the Green Chapel in the fourteenth century poem *Sir Gawain and the Green Knight*, part of the Arthurian cycle.

Lud's Church.
Mark Titterton

King Arthur also appears in a story told about Alderley Edge, on the far fringes of the Peak District in Cheshire. The story goes that a local farmer was leading a white horse to market in Macclesfield. As he approached a cave on the wooded escarpment of Alderley Edge, known as Thieves' Hollow, he met a robed and bearded old man who offered to buy the horse. Believing he could obtain a better price at the market the farmer refused and continued on his way.

However, he failed to sell the horse, and walking despondently home at the end of the day he passed the same cave and was accosted by the same old man making the same offer. With nothing to lose this time, the farmer accepted the old man's price and was led off the path to a large rock. The old man struck the rock with his staff, and it opened up to reveal a deep cavern.

The farmer followed the old man inside, and was astonished to see King Arthur and his knights in silver armour, all sleeping alongside their white horses. However, the number of horses was one short, and the farmer's horse was needed to make up the number. The old man paid the agreed price in golden treasure and the farmer left the cave, the rock closing behind him. In future years he tried many times to find the place again, but he never could.

The Welsh warrior-poet Llywarch is connected with Carl Wark, the impressive Iron Age hillfort on Hathersage Moor which dominates the skyline for miles around. It is suggested that Llywarch was the lord here, ruling the southern part of the ancient kingdom of Rheged and fighting a terrible battle with a foreign army which invaded after Roman army of occupation withdrew in the fifth century. After holding out for a long and bitter period at Carl Wark, Llywarch and his forces were finally driven from the defensive outcrop, but Llywarch went on to live for many years and become one of the four Welsh master bards (the others being Myrddin, Taliesin and Aneirin).

Finally in this section, certain communities in the Peaks remember connections to heroes and villains long after their deaths. The village of Castleton, beneath the slopes of the brooding Mam Tor, remembers the restoration of King Charles II in 1660, celebrating on Oak Apple Day (May 29, so-called because the deposed king famously hid from Roundhead troops in an oak tree).

The villagers create an elaborate bell-shaped garland of flowers, reputed to weigh up to sixty pounds, which is worn by an elected member of the community who becomes the Garland King. The garland is so big that only the King's legs are visible as he processes around the village on horseback, accompanied by dancers and musicians and stopping at the various pubs along the way. Eventually he arrives at the churchyard gate, where the garland is removed and hoisted to the pinnacle of the church tower. It remains there for a few days before being brought down and the frame stored for next year.

WITCHES AND THE DEVIL

Ladybower Reservoir.
iStock

As in other areas of Britain, the Devil is often held responsible for landscape features and rock formations. One such is the Devil's Coach and Horses, a group of weathered sandstone stacks on Derwent Edge; a local story connects them with Cutthroat Bridge, near Ladybower Reservoir in the valley below.

One day a local farmer was dipping his sheep in the river by the bridge when another man arrived with his own flock. The newcomer watched for a while, and was clearly impressed by the farmer's skill, for he said, "Will you dip my sheep, too, since you're so good at it?"

The local man was not keen on working for nothing for a stranger who appeared to be too lazy to do the job himself. He asked for payment, upon which the newcomer produced a bag of gold from beneath his black cloak. "I'll be glad to pay you for your trouble," he smiled.

The farmer still wasn't sure, having caught a distinct whiff of brimstone from the stranger and his animals, but the lure of the gold was too strong; he agreed to the bargain, and started to dip the sheep.

Before long, however, the Devil (for it was he) grew tired of waiting and threw off his disguise. With a hideous laugh he turned his sheep into a coach and horses and then drove the vehicle at breakneck speed up onto Derwent Edge. There he vanished and the coach and horses were turned to stone, where they still form part of the skyline.

The final detail, however, is that the poor farmer was so disturbed by what he had experienced that he cut his own throat, right there on the bridge – hence its name, Cutthroat Bridge. However, no diabolical gold was ever found, either in his pockets or anywhere nearby.

Hills and valleys in the Dark Peak, near Glossop.
iStock

The Devil's Dyke, near Glossop in the far north-west of Derbyshire, also has clear connections with Old Nick. Local legend goes that there once lived a man in the valley of Mossy Lea, in a house hard by the drove road linking Glossop and Sheffield. He was wealthy, and was learned in medicine and philosophy. However, rumours in the local area whispered that he was also skilled in the darker arts, having sold his soul to the Devil in order to benefit from unearthly powers and knowledge. He was known in the area as a wizard or conjuror, as well as a doctor.

When the time came for the Devil to take his due, he arrived at the doctor's house mounted on a fine black horse and demanded his soul in payment for all the years of knowledge and wealth. The doctor had been expecting him, however, and was prepared.

"Yes, yes," he replied, "I'm ready. But first, do let me admire your fine horse. What a splendid beast! I declare, I believe it might almost be as fast as my bay mare."

The Devil was proud of his steed and reacted indignantly. "Almost? My horse can outpace any mortal animal!"

"Well!" smiled the doctor. "That sounds like a challenge. I propose a wager — a race from here, along the road, and then upstream along the brook to the bank of the clough. Whoever gets there first is the winner."

The Devil snorted. "And what will you wager? Your soul is already mine!"

"Why, all my books, my instruments, my magical tools and my lifelong store of knowledge. And if I win, of course, I'll claim my soul back."

The Devil couldn't resist the challenge, as the doctor knew he wouldn't, and very shortly the race was on.

They galloped along the drove road and then off over the moor, following the line of the brook. At first the horses were equally matched, but soon the Devil's stallion began to pull ahead, and the Devil laughed triumphantly.

The doctor was not so easily beaten, however. Leaning forward in his saddle he whispered a spell into his mare's ear, and she found a new burst of speed. As they came up close behind the Devil's mount he leaned forward again and grabbed the Devil's tail, yanking it hard. The bay mare drew level with the stallion; the doctor repeated his spell and pulled the Devil's tail again, and his mare edged past and into the lead just as they reached the bank of the clough. The doctor had won.

The Devil was enraged by his defeat. Bellowing in fury, he gouged a deep trench in the earth with his claw. This ditch can be seen to this day, and is known as the Devil's Dyke. Furthermore, the drove road which crosses the moor, along which the doctor and the Devil raced, is still known as Doctor's Gate.

Another landscape feature which has a connection with the Devil is Peak Cavern near Castleton, the largest showcave system in the Peak District. Now open to visitors, once it was regarded as a wonder of the world, a gateway to the mythical land of the fairies, and the source of all the wind in the area. An alternative name for the cavern is the Devil's Arse, implying that the Prince of Darkness must be a flatulent fellow indeed.

Eldon Hole.
Harry Parker (courtesy of the Peak District Lead Mining Museum)

Peak Cavern.
Harry Parker (courtesy of the Peak District Lead Mining Museum)

It was believed that the Peak Cavern system joined with another cave, Eldon Hole in the Peak Forest, also thought to be frequented by the Devil. In a bid to test this underground connection, some locals decided to send a goose into Eldon Hole, watching as it disappeared into the darkness. Some two days later it did indeed emerge from the Devil's Arse – with its feathers singed!

Of course, the Devil also interacted with buildings, most notably the Church of Saint Mary and All Saints in Chesterfield. This church is known for its crooked spire, which has become the emblem of the town, and one local legend suggests that the crook in the spire was caused by the Devil, who was enraged when a local blacksmith managed to hammer horseshoes on his feet and dealt it a savage kick as he flew past. Another version of the story suggests that Old Nick alighted on the spire for a rest, wrapping his tail around it for balance. After a while the smell of the incense wafting up from the services got up his nose, causing him to sneeze and knock the spire sideways.

More prosaically, it is possible that the wooden frame supporting the spire has warped since it was built. However it happened, the spire has been bent and twisted for many years – although some suggest it will miraculously right itself on the day that a virgin couple gets married in the church below...

The crooked spire at Chesterfield's Church of Saint Mary and All Saints.
iStock

Witches had an evil reputation in the past, but it is likely that many of the individuals we read about had simply aroused the jealousy or suspicion of their neighbours in some way. In times that were rife with superstition, and encouraged by a puritan and fanatical church that denounced witchcraft in all its forms, it would have been easy to blame chance misfortune on an eccentric neighbour. Maybe a churn of soured milk was caused by the crazy old lady next door who talked to her plants and kept a cat, or perhaps a charm provided by the local healer or wise woman failed to work its magic, leading the disgruntled client to want revenge or reparation. In any case, down the centuries many individuals were charged with witchcraft by their neighbours, and some were executed for it.

In the Peak District, perhaps the best known of these cases was that of the Bakewell Witches. In 1608 a Scottish vagrant was found in a London cellar, penniless and minus most of his clothes. When brought before the magistrates he claimed that his clothes and other possessions were in the house of a Mrs Stafford of Bakewell, in Derbyshire. Upon questioning, he told the following extraordinary tale.

He claimed to have lodged in Bakewell the previous night in the house of the widowed Mrs Stafford, which she shared with her sister. The women were milliners, but not prosperous, supplementing their meagre income by offering lodging to travellers. After retiring to bed, claimed the Scotsman, he had been awakened by noises from the room below, and he had peeked through a crack in the floorboards and witnessed Mrs Stafford and her sister uttering the following incantation: "O'er thick, o'er thin, now Devil, to th' cellar in Lunnon." As they said these words they disappeared and the light went out.

Naturally puzzled, the Scotsman turned over the events in his mind, muttering the incantation under his breath – upon which he felt himself lifted and rushed through the air, eventually landing in a cellar beside the two women. They were busy tying up bundles of expensive cloth, which he supposed they had stolen; after a short while they noticed him and gave him wine to drink, and after a time he fell into a drunken sleep, knowing no more until he was found by the night watchman.

The magistrate immediately suspected witchcraft, and ordered a search of Mrs Stafford's house in Bakewell. Sure enough the Scotsman's clothes and possessions were found, and the two women were arrested. Their explanation was that the Scotsman had indeed lodged with them for several days, but he had proved to be unable to pay his rent, so they had evicted him and kept some of his clothes and belongings in lieu of payment. He had gone on his way to London, and had probably ended up sleeping in the cellar because he couldn't afford other lodgings.

Reasonable as this sounds, it did the women no good; they were taken to Derby Assizes, tried for witchcraft, found guilty and hanged. Genuine witchcraft, or an angry man's revenge on two honest women? At this distance, it is impossible to know for certain.

The bridge over the River Wye at Bakewell.
iStock

Another witch once lived at Swythamley, north of Leek in Staffordshire. Apparently this woman was known to be able to turn into a particularly swift hare, and her husband made an arrangement with a local farmer that he could course her with his dogs in return for a monetary fee. The witch's husband evidently enjoyed watching the sport enormously; whether the witch herself knew about this arrangement between her husband and her neighbour (and if so, what she thought of it) is not recorded. However, her existence is remembered in the name of Old Hag Farm in the parish.

BLACK DOGS, RAMS AND OTHER STRANGE BEASTS

Across the UK there are legends and tales of ghostly animals, usually appearing to solitary travellers on isolated roads. These apparitions are almost always black, usually of gigantic size, and can take the form of dogs, pigs or occasionally donkeys. They are most often interpreted as a portent or warning of some kind – although occasionally they are helpful, acting as guides to help lost individuals get home safely.

The lead mining village of Bradwell was once home to one of the Peak District's black dogs, which in this case seems to have appeared as a warning. Two brothers, both miners, were walking home from the pub late one night when one of them stopped in his tracks. A huge black hound, eyes glowing, was padding up to him – but his brother was unable to see the beast, and accused him of being in his cups. The dog vanished as suddenly as it had appeared, leaving the first brother badly shaken and convinced he had received a warning.

The next morning the two brothers got up for work in the mine as usual, but the one that had seen the dog had second thoughts and decided not to go to work that day. He was wise to heed the warning; there was a tragic collapse in the mine, and his brother was killed.

A pack of spectral dogs known as the Gabriel Hounds is thought to gallop wildly across the Peak District skies on stormy nights. Their belling is generally taken as a portent of death, either for the person who hears them or for someone in their household, or else as a sign of some great impending catastrophe – war, plague, famine or natural disaster. They are also sometimes thought to pursue wrongdoers, running them down until they are exhausted and then escorting their souls to the underworld. In Derbyshire they are associated with an impious local landowner who persisted in hunting on the Sabbath and once even drove his pack of hounds into the local church during a service. For this sacrilege he was condemned to ride forever on windy nights, driving his baying hounds before him.

Another dog-like – or possibly wolf-like – creature has been seen near Wormhill, east of Buxton in the High Peak, running and leaping with unnatural speed at vehicles travelling along the local roads. Tradition suggests that this apparition is connected with the slaying of the last wolf in England, attributed to the ancient

Wolfhunte family who once held lands here by virtue of their skill at hunting wolves in the royal forests. It seems the last wolf may still be bearing a grudge — as well he might.

Less ghostly sightings of unusual beasts relate to a population of wallabies that was released from Swythamley Hall during the Second World War, and which established itself in the region of the gritstone escarpment of the Roaches and Ramshaw Rocks, near Leek. They were spotted regularly in the 1960s, but numbers have dwindled since then and the last sighting was some time ago — but rumours persist that a few secretive individuals may still survive.

Ramshaw Rocks, near Leek. Keep an eye out for wallabies...
iStock

There are also some animal legends associated with the Chesterfield area. One suggests that the town was once menaced by a rampaging cow, which had been enchanted by a local witch and was laying waste to the countryside. The townsfolk engaged the services of a knight who had been to the Crusades and was therefore not fazed by a mere cow; sure enough he despatched the creature with little effort, and its bones were displayed as proof that the deed had been done. One apparently still remains, resting on a tomb in Chesterfield church.

The tale of the Derby Ram (or the Old Tup, as he is sometimes known) is one of the oldest folk tales associated with the Derby area, immortalised in a song which is part of the repertoire of many folk singers and which has been recorded in a number of versions down the years. The story tells that a traveller on his way to market in Derby encountered a ram of gargantuan proportions; the song goes on to list the beast's various body parts and describe how enormous they were, both while it was alive and after it had been butchered. A few of the verses go as follows:

> *As I was going to Derby, sir,*
> *All on a market day,*
> *I met the finest Ram, Sir,*
> *That ever was fed on hay.*

> *Daddle-i-day, daddle-i-day,*
> *Fal-de-ral, fal-de-ral, daddle-i-day.*

> *This ram was fat behind, sir,*
> *This ram was fat before,*
> *This ram was ten yards high, sir,*
> *Indeed he was no more.*

> *Daddle-i-day, etc.*

> *The butcher that killed this ram, sir,*
> *Was drownded in the blood,*
> *And the boy that held the pail, sir,*
> *Was carried away in the flood.*

> *Daddle-i-day, etc.*

The Derby RAM sculpture in Derby city centre.

The ram has been associated with Derby for centuries; the football team are known as the Rams and use a version of the song as their anthem, and various Derbyshire regiments down the years have used a ram as their mascot. There is even a sculpture of a ram in Derby city centre shopping area – a reminder to the shopping public, although it is debatable how many of them are aware of the Old Tup's ancient association with the city.

HAUNTINGS AND CURSES

Many places in the Peaks are known to be haunted, and some are also thought to be cursed. Ghosts, the supernatural and the power of curses and maledictions were only too real to our rural ancestors, and a number of places developed sinister reputations, sometimes because of the atmosphere of the places themselves but in many cases because of the events that occurred there.

Magpie Mine.
Mark Titterton

One such is Magpie Mine, an abandoned lead mine high on the bleak limestone plateau near the village of Sheldon. First opened in 1740, the working initially prospered, but in 1824 there was a dispute between Magpie men and the miners in the neighbouring

Maypitt and Redsoil Mines over the rights to the rich veins of lead which ran through the entire area. Over a number of years claims and counter-claims were submitted to the local Barmote Court, but no resolution was reached and tensions ran high.

Then in 1833 an explosion in the Magpie workings injured a Maypitt worker, and the situation tipped over into active aggression. The miners launched a tit-for-tat campaign of smoking each other out by lighting fires underground, culminating in the deaths of three Redsoil men who died from smoke inhalation. Ten Magpie men were charged in connection with the deaths, but were acquitted due to the clever arguments of their lawyer.

The Redsoil faction, especially the widows of the dead men, were enraged, and one of the widows pronounced a curse on the Magpie Mine which apparently took immediate hold; the mine never again turned a profit, despite heavy investment from a series of wealthy backers. Indeed, some of these backers went bankrupt, and the curse was blamed for a number of accidents and deaths that occurred at the mine. It was also said to be haunted; miners in the 1940s reported seeing a figure which a candle which disappeared as they approached.

The mine struggled on against its bad reputation and worse profits until 1954, when it finally closed. The surface buildings still stand on the moor near Sheldon, managed by the Peak District Mines Historical Society; this is now a quiet and peaceful spot, but it doesn't take much imagination to repopulate it with the activities and conflicts of past times.

Like sailors, miners have always been superstitious, even in the absence of murders and curses. In St Mary's Church in Wirksworth can be seen a tiny carving of a lead miner, complete with pick and kibble (or basket). The carving, known as "T'Owd Man", may have Anglo-Saxon origins, and he is thought to have been a talisman for the local industrial workers.

Wirksworth is not his original home, however; he was found during a restoration of the thirteenth century Church of St James in Bonsall, appropriated and taken to Wirksworth where he is now firmly mortared into the church wall. The feelings of the Bonsall miners about this highjacking of their good-luck charm may only be imagined.

T'Owd Man.
Mark Titterton

Mines were often thought to be inhabited by mischievous and sometimes malicious spirits, who caused unexplained lights and sounds (voices, bangs or taps), blew candles or lamps out and sometimes lured unwary miners to their deaths. One such entity was known locally as the Knockerdown, who was known to cause timber supports to fail, triggering underground collapses and accidents.

The Nine Ladies stone circle is a beautiful and atmospheric site, standing on Stanton Moor near the village of Stanton in the Peak – but here also some local villagers apparently fell victim to a magical curse, although this time it was religious in origin. The

The Nine Ladies stone circle, dancing forever on Stanton Moor.
iStock

story goes that a girl from Stanton village fell in love with a local lad and they became betrothed. The girl was so excited about the match that she took several of her friends up onto the moor one Saturday to dance in celebration, persuading an elderly man from the village to bring his fiddle to play for them.

The young women danced and the fiddler played, on and on into the afternoon and evening. They were all having such a fine time that they did not notice as the sun set and night drew in; the moon rose and the stars came out, but they played and danced on, until eventually the church clock in the village below the moor struck midnight and the day changed from Saturday to Sunday.

Now, as every god-fearing villager knew, dancing and celebrating on a Sunday was a sin – but the merry-making continued, until eventually the ladies were turned to stone as they danced, and the fiddler with them. They stand there still, the ladies in their circle and the fiddler standing by himself off to the side.

Finally in this section, the wild and lonely Winnats Pass, on the road west out of Castleton, is a spectacular and steep limestone gorge that has been the site of many stories and legends. The most famous is the story of Henry and Clara, a betrothed couple who were travelling to be married in the Peak Forest Chapel. At that time the vicar in Peak Forest was able to perform weddings without the usual reading of the banns, and indeed without the permission of the bride and groom's family; the village was known as the Gretna Green of Derbyshire. The story goes that Clara's family had objected to her choice of husband since she was of noble blood and he was not, but the lovers decided to take matters into their own hands and elope.

On their way to Peak Forest they stopped for refreshment at an inn in Castleton, where they were noticed by a group of five lead miners. The men noted the couple's rich clothing, overheard them asking directions to Peak Forest, and surmised that they were probably carrying a large sum of money with them so they could pay the vicar.

The couple soon set out again, but the miners had gone ahead and lay in wait near the head of Winnats Pass, where the road is at its steepest and most narrow. There was no escape for poor Henry and Clara; ignoring their desperate entreaties the miners cut his throat and beat her to death with a pickaxe. Their bodies were dumped in a mineshaft and the murderers went on their way.

Winnats Pass.

Henry and Clara were not discovered for many years, despite their families' efforts to trace them. However, the miners did not enjoy the fruits of their crime; of the five, only one lived into old age. One was killed in a mining accident, another fell to his death in Winnats Pass, one committed suicide and the fourth died mad. The bodies of the couple were only located when the fifth man made a deathbed confession – but it is said that their spirits remain in Winnats Pass, forever together but forever pleading in vain for their lives.

HOBS, GIANTS, FAIRIES AND OTHER SPIRITS OF PLACE

Hobs are natural spirits who live in the wild places, often making their homes in woods, caves or in the vicinity of rock formations or ancient monuments such as the mighty stone circle of Arbor Low on Middleton Moor, near Youlgrave. One such lives in the Bronze Age burial cist known as Hob Hurst's House, on Beeley Moor above the Chatsworth Estate. A story tells that this hob once helped out a poor cobbler and his family by calling at the man's house in the dead of night and making shoes. The next day the man sold the shoes and bought more leather, and the next night Hob Hurst turned it into more pairs of shoes. The cycle continued at a faster and faster rate until the cobbler could no longer keep up with the hob; the house became filled with unsold shoes and the hob was forced to throw them out of the window as he finished them. This story is thought to have given rise to a saying in the Sheffield area, aimed at someone who can produce goods at a prodigious rate: "Tha can mek 'em faster than Hob Hurst can throw shoes out o' t' window."

Hob Hurst merely visited the cobbler in the story above — like the hob who lives in Monsal Dale on the flanks of the Iron Age hillfort of Fin Cop, who visits farmhouses throughout the dale to perform threshing, cleaning and other menial physical tasks. Others confine themselves to their homes, like the hob of Thor's

Hob Hurst's House.
Karl Barton

Cave, high above the River Manifold, who appears to be fond of music and whose fiddle can sometimes be heard screeching from the cave. However, hobs can sometimes be persuaded to take up permanent residence in houses or on farms, making themselves useful by doing housework, churning milk and keeping an eye on the livestock. They often like some form of payment in the form of food and drink left out for them each evening by the grateful householders.

One young farmer from Chelmorton was aware of this, and so he blessed his luck when he came across a hob sitting by the side of the road as he walked home late one evening. The farmer lived alone and saw an opportunity to make his life easier – a clean and tidy house and help around the farm, all for the price of a bit of food and drink each evening! So he crept up on the hob and grabbed it, bundling it into an empty sack and then setting off for home.

The hob was unhappy to be captured, though, and soon set up a terrible wailing and complaining. It pleaded with its captor to let it go, and soon its heart-wrenching cries touched the farmer's conscience. He took pity on the poor creature, set the sack down and untied the top, at which the little fellow leapt out and scampered off to take refuge in its home, a cave in Deep Dale just below Topley Pike near the village of King Sterndale. The cave is known today as Thirst House, and a spring outside was thought to have been charmed by the hob in gratitude to the farmer for letting him go; anyone drinking from it on Good Friday will have all their ailments cured.

Another hob, or perhaps a dwarf, is the little red hairy man who is associated with a lead mining tale from Youlgrave. A miner from the village had three sons, but the family was poor and the sons dreamed of making their fortunes. One day the eldest son had had enough of the filthy and dangerous work of lead mining, and set out to find his fortune. He walked for half a day, and then sat in the shade of a small wood to eat his lunch. As he unpacked his bread and cheese a little red hairy man appeared and begged for a share of the food, but the lad refused and told him to be off. After his meal the young man continued on his way, but despite his best efforts he failed to find his fortune, and within a few weeks he was back at home.

However, this did not deter the middle son, who decided to try his own luck. He set off as his brother had done, and after walking for a few hours he sat in the same shady wood to eat his lunch. The same little red hairy man appeared and begged for a share of the victuals – but this lad was a bit more generous than his brother, and he threw the little man some crumbs of bread and the rind of his cheese. The man ate what he was offered, and then told the lad that if he wanted to find his fortune he should look in the centre of the wood.

Full of hope, the lad searched the wood and came across an abandoned lead mine. However, it looked old and worked-out, and anyway, he was trying to get away from lead mining, so he went on his way. Needless to say, he fared no better than his brother, and in a few weeks' time he also was back at home with his family, no better off.

Undaunted, the youngest son thought he might do better, so he said his goodbyes and set out. On his first day of walking he came to the same shady wood and sat to eat his lunch, and the same little red hairy man appeared, begging for food. This lad was much more generous than his brothers, and he shared his bread and cheese equally with the little man.

When they had finished eating the little man gave the same advice to him that he had given to the middle brother – the lad's fortune would be found at the centre of the wood. After some searching he located the same abandoned lead mine, but the little man was waiting for him and told him to get in a basket to be lowered down into the mine.

Rather trustingly, the youngest son did as he was bid – and at the bottom of the shaft he found himself in an open, bright and beautiful landscape. Again the little red hairy man was waiting for him, and guided him through a series of adventures to defeat three giants and rescue a princess, who (naturally) agreed to be his wife. Eventually the lad returned home with all the riches of the three giants' castles and a princess on his arm, to live happily and prosperously in Youlgrave until the end of his days.

Like most other areas of the country, the Peak District has its share of giants who are held to be responsible for (or sometimes to be) large landscape features. One such is Hulac Warren who once lived

Youlgrave.

near Fin Cop. At that time the hillfort on the Cop was inhabited by a powerful clan who farmed and hunted the surrounding countryside, and for many years all was peaceful.

Hulac would often watch the clan members going about their activities, and one day he caught sight of Hedessa, a shepherd girl who was famed for her beauty. He determined on the spot to have Hedessa for himself, and made several approaches to her, but she was put off by his hideous ugliness and called on the clan's gods to protect her. This they did — for a while.

However, one evening Hulac lay in wait for Hedessa as she returned home, seized her and carried her off to his lair in the rocks at the top of a nearby escarpment. Hedessa wept bitterly and implored the gods to deliver her, but in the end she delivered herself by breaking free from the giant's embrace and throwing herself down the rockface to her death.

Hulac was enraged to be cheated of his prize and cursed the gods for their cruelty. Hearing him, the gods took rather belated action, turning him to stone and hurling him into the River Wye in Monsal Dale. There he still lies, a large stone with the waters of the river swirling around him. Meanwhile, at the place where Hedessa's body fell to the riverbank below a spring burst forth, thought to be watered by her tears of fear and grief. It still flows to this day, and is known locally as the Hedess Spring.

There are many fairy myths associated with locations in the Peak District – mounds, hills or solitary trees are commonly linked to the Fair Folk, who are often ambivalent in their dealing with mortals. One legend relates to a farm near Baslow, which contained a hill on which grew three tall trees. Locals reported that they had heard singing and laughter from the hilltop, and had caught glimpses of three fairy women dressed in green dancing around the treetrunks. The hilltop was shunned by most folk – apart from the farmer, who ascended the hill every Midsummer's Eve and left a gift of flowers against each tree.

The waters of the River Wye in Monsal Dale – fed by Hedessa's tears?
iStock

His farm prospered, until his death when the land was divided between his three sons. One, the youngest, kept up the tradition of leaving floral offerings for the green ladies, although his brothers scoffed at him – but his farm prospered while the others did not.

Eventually the two foolish brothers decided to end the tradition by cutting down the trees. They took their axes to the top of the hill, but when they bit into the treetrunks the sounds of women screaming were heard. However, the brothers persevered and two of the trees were felled, but the ladies had their revenge – the falling trunks crushed the brothers where they stood, although they had taken care to stand out of the way.

The youngest brother inherited all the land, and he continued to take his midsummer gift of flowers to the last remaining tree on One Tree Hill. His farm continued to do well, but no more laughter and singing were heard from the hilltop, and the single figure of a lonely green lady could sometimes be seen standing sadly by her tree.

Fairies are also known to dance on a hill at Cauldon Low, near Ashbourne, perhaps associated with the prehistoric tumuli that used to exist there. These fairies are kindly folk, for it is recorded in a song that they are engaged with helping the inhabitants of the local area and putting right all their problems.

A rather closer encounter with the fair folk was granted to a preacher from Ashbourne, who had agreed to preach a sermon at Hartington but was delayed on his journey, first when his horse went lame so he had to walk, and then by losing his way on the moors when a storm broke. As night fell and the storm showed no signs of abating, the minister was forced to seek shelter in a remote and tumbledown cottage inhabited by an elderly couple.

They took him in gladly, but had no food to give him, and they warned him that the house was haunted and he might hear noises in the night. Sure enough, after he and his hosts had retired to sleep he heard the sounds of food preparation downstairs, and then a voice calling, "Armaley, Armaley, come to thy supper!"

At the mention of supper the hungry minister got out of bed and went downstairs, and was surprised to find a large gathering of beautiful and richly dressed people, all sitting down to eat at a table groaning with fine food. They invited him to join them, so he took a place at the table and closed his eyes to say grace. However, the prayer included the words "All devils, fear and fly!" – and when the minister opened his eyes the people, the table and all the fine food had vanished.

POOLS, RIVERS AND OTHER WATER SOURCES

It might seem odd for the land-locked Peak District to boast a small collection of mermaids, but the Staffordshire moorlands are said to be home to three of the creatures (or perhaps just one with three homes). The first is at Doxey Pool, a body of water some fifteen metres by ten metres which lies at the top of the Roaches

Blake Mere Pool, near Leek.
iStock

above Leek and the Tittesworth Reservoir. This mermaid is a long way from the beautiful singing creatures of maritime legend; known as Jenny Greenteeth, she is hideous and hostile, said to rise from the depths, dripping and draped in weed and slime, to terrify anyone who dares to swim in her pool.

The second mermaid lives at Blake Mere (or the Mermaid's Pool), another natural pond about six miles northwest of Leek. It is said that no beast will drink from this pool, no bird will fly over it, and no fish live in its brackish water. The mermaid who resides here is less terrifying than Jenny Greenteeth, but no less dangerous; she is said to rise at midnight and call out to anyone who happens to be by the side of the pool, luring them towards her. Far from friendly, though, she then drags them down into the depths of the pond to join her in her watery home. A poem on display in the local pub confirms this:

The Derwent at Cromford.
Mark Titterton

> *She calls on you to greet her, Combing her dripping crown,*
> *But if you go to meet her, She ups and drags you down.*

The final mermaid is more benevolent. She lives not in a pond but in a cave hidden in the rocks on the slopes of Kinder Scout, and every day she emerges to bathe in the pool nearby. It is said that she grants long life to anyone who sees her – but she has also been known to lure swimmers to their deaths in the waters of her pool.

All three of these pools are said to be bottomless and never run dry, and some say that they are all connected by an underground tunnel and the mermaid flits between the three locations. Whether this is true or not, there is no denying that all three places have an eerie atmosphere all their own.

The River Derwent rises at Bleaklow near Glossop and meanders south for over sixty miles, flowing through the heart of the Peak District to join the Trent near Shardlow. Inevitably it has collected many stories and myths along its way – in some regions it is regarded almost as a living thing, able to punish those who show it disrespect. A tale from Cromford, where the Derwent flows swift and deep, recounts that the river rose up and drowned an individual who had referred to it as "nought but a brook".

Just downstream from Cromford is the village of Whatstandwell (formerly Whatstandwell Bridge). The story of the village's curious name goes that there was once a man named Walter (or Wat) Stonewall, who lived by the Derwent in the late fourteenth century in a house owned by Darley Abbey. At that time there was a ford crossing the river at the point where the modern A6 road bridge now stands; Walter Stonewall manned the ford, which was used by monks travelling between Darley Abbey and their property at Wigwell Grange.

Then, in or around 1391 a certain John de Stepul, a landowner from Bolehill in Wirksworth, undertook to build a bridge at the fording point as an act of piety (and presumably so the monks wouldn't get their cassocks wet crossing the river). An agreement between de Stepul and the Abbot of Darley Abbey was drawn up, the bridge was duly built, and it became known as Wat Stonewall's Bridge after the crossing keeper who still lived in his house nearby. Over the intervening years the name has corrupted into the form in use today.

There are three reservoirs in the Derwent's upper reaches, Howden, Derwent and Ladybower, built to provide a reliable supply of water for much of Derbyshire as well as parts of South Yorkshire and as far afield as Nottingham and Leicester. The creation of this string of artificial lakes inevitably caused the loss of land and settlements; there was once a Derwent village under the reservoir of the same name, where a vicar is said to have seen his own face staring back at him as he preached the annual Sermon for the Dead, when all the souls of those fated to die in the coming year would gather to listen. This must have been something of a shock, but nevertheless he gamely carried on with the service — and sure enough, the story tells that he was dead within a year.

As elsewhere, there were once many wells in Derbyshire, built to harness natural springs or underground watercourses and provide reliable water for the local population. Most of these are static affairs, with water levels remaining more or less constant — but a rare few possess the quality of ebbing and flowing, appearing almost tidal. There was one of these at Tideswell; although it has now lost its fluctuating character, it was once known as a wonder of the Peak, and it can still be seen in a garden in the north of the village. Indeed, some believe this "tidal well" provides the origin of the village's name, although this is disputed.

LEGENDS & FOLKLORE THE PEAK DISTRICT

Well dressing, Tissington.
Mark Titterton

Of course, the best-known water-related custom in the Peak District is well dressing. This summertime community tradition involves creating elaborate pictorial decorations out of natural items such as petals, seeds and moss, to be placed by wells, fountains, springs or street taps as part of a week of celebrations and events. It is almost unique to the Staffordshire and Derbyshire moorland area, and in its earliest form it is thought to constitute a folk-memory of Pagan days when water spirits were venerated for their life-sustaining powers.

The village of Tissington claims to be the home of well dressing in its current form, with some suggesting that the tradition dates back to the plague years of 1348–9, when many villages and hamlets were decimated but Tissington was left largely untouched. The villagers ascribed their miraculous escape to the purity of their water supply, and gave thanks by decorating the village wells with flowers and garlands. The well dressing tradition grew from this small beginning to become part of the annual round of village celebrations in most Peak District settlements.

The creation of the dressings is a communal affair, involving many hours of labour and effort. The resulting displays are stunning, often commemorating local events, relating to current affairs or reflecting religious scenes. They are blessed by the local priest, who processes around visiting each site in turn, and then usually the whole village celebrates with fairs, carnivals, sporting competitions and other events.

SUPERSTITIONS AND OMENS

The uncertainty and precariousness of life in bygone centuries meant that signs, symbols and superstitions were given great importance. Life was ruled by observations and omens, and the closeness of our rural ancestors' relationship with the natural world around them meant that many of these proverbs referred to the behaviour of plants, animals and even the weather – and some were in rhyming form, perhaps to aid the memory. For example:

Hawthorn bloom and elder flowers

Will fill a house with evil powers

When old cats play, rain is on the way

If there's ice in November to hold a duck,

There will be a winter of slush and muck

If the moon on a Saturday be new or full,

There always was rain and there always will.

Onion skins very thin: a mild winter coming in.

Onion skins thick and tough: coming winter wild and rough.

If spiders are many and spinning their webs, the weather will soon be very dry.

When pine cones open on the trees, the weather is set fine.

Oak before ash – we're in for a splash;

Ash before oak – we're in for a soak.

Mam Tor.
iStock

Household activities were set about with superstitions of all kinds. A hat on a bed brought bad luck, while a candle flickering or burning with a blue flame indicated the presence of a spirit in the room. Other proverbs and sayings related to commerce or education (although they may not be taken as the truth nowadays!). For example:

> *He that buys land buys many stones,*
> *He that buys flesh buys many bones,*
> *He that buys eggs buys many shells,*
> *But he that buys good ale buys nothing else.*

A cow, a sow and a woman – you can learn them nothing,

A dog, a horse and a man – you can learn them anything.

The harvesting of certain crops was thought to be related to the phase of the moon, as shown in this rhyme:

When the moon is at the full,

Mushrooms you may freely pull;

But when the moon is on the wane,

Wait 'ere you think to pluck again.'

Moonrise over Derbyshire.
iStock

GOOD LUCK, BAD LUCK

According to our rural ancestors, if you want to avoid bad luck for yourself or someone else you should avoid doing the following:

Walking under a ladder

Putting shoes or boots on the table

Shaking hands across the dinner table

Spilling salt on the table

Singing at the table

Sleeping on the table

Placing your knife and fork crossways on your plate

Turning your bed on a Sunday

Brushing the dust out of the front door

Giving gloves as a present

Cutting your fingernails on a Monday, Friday or Sunday

Opening an umbrella in the house

Bringing thyme into the house

Carrying anything on your shoulder in the house

Entering a house for the first time through the back door

Throwing dead flowers onto the fire

Cutting down a flowering tree

Turning back after beginning a journey

Doing anything on Friday 13th

Nailing up a horseshoe with the points down (all the luck will drain out)

Killing a sparrow (they carry the souls of the dead)

Breaking a mirror

Treading on a grave

Leaving a house by a different door from the one you used to enter

Giving a gift of an empty purse or wallet (it should always contain a little money)

Likewise, to ensure good luck you should:

Carry a piece of coal in your pocket

Carry a piece of iron with a hole in it

Carry a rabbit's foot

Keep a lock of hair from a baby's first haircut

Burn your tea leaves

Salute a solitary magpie

Wish on a falling star

Bow nine times to the new moon

Cut your fingernails on a Thursday

Put on your left sock or stocking first when getting dressed

Pick up a pin if you see one

Pick up a white stone, spit on it and throw it over your head

Take a snail by its horns and throw it backwards over your shoulder

Throw a pinch of salt over your left shoulder

Begin a journey with your right foot first

Look for a four-leaved clover

Look for a double-leaved sprig of ash

If you see a penny or a pin on the ground, always pick it up

Let a black cat cross your path

Nail up a horseshoe with the points upwards (to keep the luck from spilling out — and always use seven nails!)

Cross your fingers if you accidentally do anything unlucky

Catch a falling leaf — the more you catch, the more good luck you will have

THE JOURNEY THROUGH LIFE

Life was more precarious in the past. A lack of understanding as to the cause of diseases or the knowledge of how to cure them meant mortality rates were high, especially among children. For the same reason, accidents involving injury were also far more serious. Wars were more frequent, too.

The perilous journey through life had important stages which were celebrated with ritual and accompanied by superstition. There were several strange beliefs regarding the beginning of life. It was said that a child born at midnight would have second sight, and that a "footling" – that is, a baby born feet first — would have magical powers. Efforts were made to preserve the caul surrounding the child at birth because it was thought to be possessed with sympathetic magic. Kept safe, it would prevent the person it belonged to from suffering death by drowning. There are records from well into the twentieth century of sailors buying cauls in the belief they would keep them safe.

As soon as a woman went into labour, a party called a Merry Meet would be held at her house. The prospective father would entertain family and neighbours, and a "groaning cheese" and a "groaning cake" would be carefully cut into exactly the right number of pieces to serve to the guests. Unfortunately, of course, the woman giving birth was unable to enjoy the festivities herself.

With infant mortality so high, it was considered essential to christen a newborn baby as soon as possible. An unbaptised child would not go to heaven if they died, and some thought they might become fairies instead. Some measure of protection could be conferred on the infant by wrapping it in its mother's clothes until the baptism could take place, or by tying a red string about its wrist. While the child was still unbaptised it was customary to make them a gift of an egg (symbolising new life), some salt and, unsafe though it may seem, a box of matches. Salt and fire were considered sure charms against the attentions of evil spirits.

If the baptism was performed at home the water used to christen the child was often thrown into the fire, to ensure it remained pure and no evil influence could pollute it. Even after baptism the infant might be at risk from fairies, who were thought to cast acquisitive eyes at human children. To ward them off, parents might hang a pair of scissors or tongs over the crib, which would dangle in the form of a cross. The cross shape and the iron in the scissors were sure protection against the little people.

If fairies did get their hands on a baby they would leave in its place a changeling, a peevish and ugly fairy child, or a block of wood enchanted to resemble the stolen infant. Babies who succumbed to what we now call Sudden Infant Death Syndrome (SIDS, or cot death) were often thought to be the lifeless substitutes left behind by kidnapping fairies.

Some mothers would bite their children's fingernails short rather than cutting them, in the belief that if they cut the fingernails the child would grow up to be a thief. It was also said that a new baby must always be carried upstairs before it goes down, otherwise it would not rise in life. If there were no stairs in the house, the midwife would climb onto a chair with it.

New mothers feared their children might be stolen by fairies unless they protected them with charms until they were baptised.

In young adulthood, there were also some interesting customs surrounding courtship. We tend to assume morals were more conservative in the past, so it may be a surprise to learn that courting couples were often allowed to sleep together undisturbed. However, this was only with the proviso that the young man kept his clothes on (minus his coat and boots). A variant custom called "bundling" allowed the couple to share a bed with a bolster between them. Such would have been the disgrace if the young couple abused this trust that few did. Mind you, engagements tended to be shorter in those days.

A young woman hoping to marry into a farming family was often called upon to prove her strength by lifting the lid of the parish chest with one arm. The parish chest was an ancient and massive locked casket kept in the church, which was used to store charitable donations and other valuables. It was usually made of thick oak, sometimes carved out of one solid piece of wood, and was usually bound with stout iron. To lift its heavy lid with one arm would be quite a feat for many men, never mind a young woman.

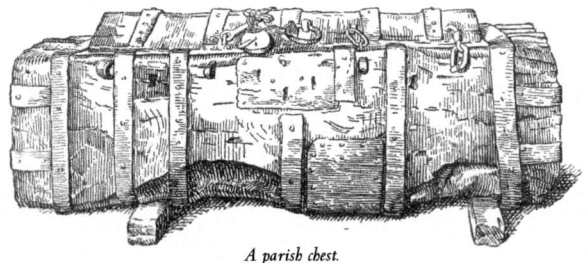

A parish chest.

As to the wedding day itself, there was an ancient custom in which the friends of the groom would call at the bride's house with a view to "abducting" her. Her duty was to hide, so as to avoid this indignity, or – better still – to sneak to the church before they caught her. This was a remnant of a much older custom in which young men would prove their worth by stealing the girl they fancied from under her parents' roof. In more civilised times, no abduction or manhandling of the bride actually took place and the whole thing was done in fun.

A rather unkind superstition related to weddings was that if a woman served as a bridesmaid three times, she would never be married herself. Likewise, a man who acted as best man three times would never wed. But there are even stranger beliefs; for example, if a young woman puts on a man's hat or a young man puts on a woman's hat, they will have to wait three years before they can get married. If a young person cuts bread obliquely or in uneven slices they will never be married, they may have to wait seven years, or else they will end up with an objectionable mother-in-law. If a girl touches the foot of another girl with a broom while sweeping, she will rob that girl of her future husband. Finally, when the bride enters the church, she must never look behind her or she will end up regretting the marriage.

There are equally strange superstitions regarding the final great change in a person's life – death. Dogs howling or owls screeching might be taken as omens of a coming death. Clocks suddenly stopping or chiming thirteen were a bad sign, as were a robin tapping at the window pane, a crow getting into the house or an owl settling on the roof. Mysterious noises such as knocks and raps in a house where someone lay ill were also ominous. Carpenters sometimes claimed they heard sounds in their workshops at night resembling those of a coffin being made. They knew then that one would soon be ordered.

When the last moment seemed to be nigh, people were sometimes "helped to die" by those looking after them. All the doors and windows in the house were opened wide to allow the soul to escape. At the same time, knots were untied, mirrors covered and the fire – the "soul of the house" – was put out. "Passing bells" were traditionally rung nine times to announce a death, but their original purpose was to scare away any evil spirits seeking to claim the soul of the departed. A plate of salt, a substance long believed to ward off evil, was placed on the body. No corpse was left with its eyes open, for it was said that it would be looking for the next person to die.

After a death, the household would keep watch for at least one night while the corpse lay in the house because it was thought that the soul of the departed might return. Sometimes the assembly would chant, "It is for the last time, it is the last night", in order

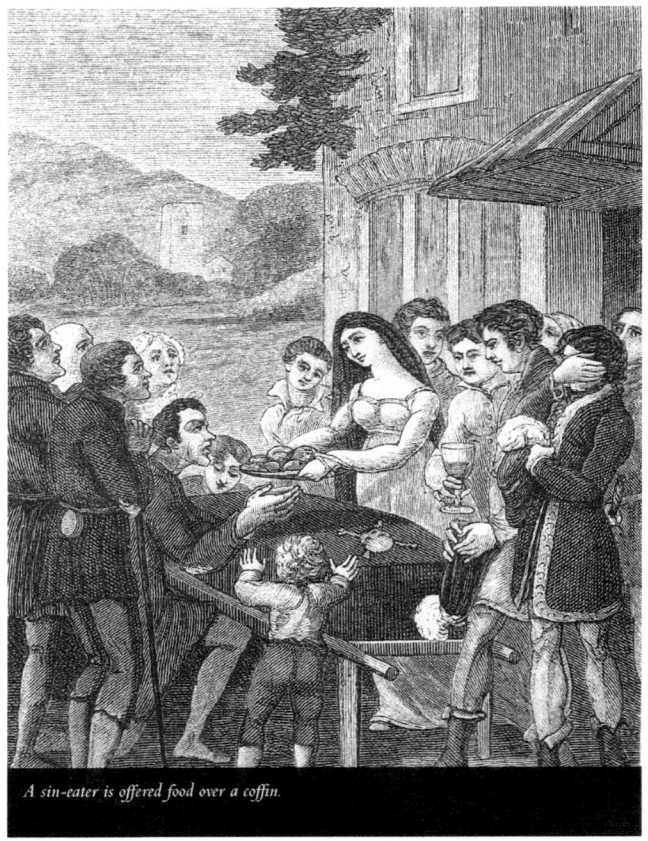
A sin-eater is offered food over a coffin.

to remind the spirit that it had to pass on. If the master of the house died it was considered important to inform the bees in the hive of the fact, otherwise they would all fly away. Any significant tree or bush, even household plants, were at one time draped with black crêpe after a death, otherwise it was feared they would wither.

When the corpse was conveyed to its burial place it had to be taken to its grave in the same direction as the sun passes through the sky – that is, "deosil" or clockwise. To take it in the opposite direction, "widdershins" or anti-clockwise, would make the soul vulnerable to malign forces. There was a prejudice about being the first person buried in a new graveyard, because it was said that the Devil had the right to claim the first corpse. Another superstition suggested that the spirit of the most recent person to be buried haunted a graveyard, watching over it until another burial took place.

A decidedly primitive custom, which had all but died out by the end of the nineteenth century, was that of the "sin-eater". The sin-eater was usually a poor member of the parish who was prepared, for a small fee and a meal, to spiritually take on the sins of a person who had just died. This would be achieved by offering them specially baked cakes, or bread on a dish of salt, the eating of which meant that he would absorb the sins. The food might even be offered over the coffin of the dead person; at any rate, the meal would always be eaten in the graveyard. This belief seems to hark back to the time when our most distant ancestors believed they could take on the power and attributes of a deceased person by devouring their body. The sin-eater was therefore a kind of spiritual cannibal.

THE WHEEL OF THE YEAR

The rural calendar was marked by a series of high days and festivals intended to mark crucial times for sowing, reaping and other agricultural activities. These were often of great antiquity, pre-dating the Christian era. Many were adopted by the church, although rededicated and renamed, and have therefore been preserved down the years.

The Celtic New Year was marked on 1 November, when winter began. The coming dark days were defied with a great celebratory feast called Samhain. Bonfires were lit, animals were mated for the following spring, and any surplus beasts were slaughtered to fatten everyone up in advance of the approaching cold. Guy Fawkes Night is a survival of the Samhain bonfire festival, merely put back a few days and given a political context which would have meant nothing to our pagan ancestors.

Known in many places as Hallows Fires, in Derbyshire the Samhain bonfires were known as Tindle Fires. Farmers lit a bonfire in a field and then carried a forkful of burning straw to the highest point on their farm, strewing the embers as far across the land as they could. Meanwhile their family would stay by the fire and pray for the souls of their departed loved ones; this tradition is recalled in occasional instances of fields with the name of Purgatory.

As a transitional period between the old year and the new, Samhain was considered a time when spirits from the underworld could revisit the earth. It was a time of ghosts and witches. This ancient belief is recalled in our modern-day Hallowe'en traditions. The church diffused the apparent menace in this festival by dedicating 1 November to all the saints in heaven. Hallows is an archaic word for saints, and Hallowe'en is a contraction of All Hallows Eve – that is, the night before All Hallows or All Saints Day. It was formerly custom around this time to go Soul Caking, roaming the parish in request of small gifts of money to be presented with specially baked dainties called soul cakes. Guisers or mummers also put on plays and entertainments, usually disguised or with their faces blackened.

The next great festival in the Celtic calendar was Imbolc, on 1 February. This marked the beginning of the lambing season and is echoed in the Christian Feast of the Purification of the Virgin Mary, or Candlemas, celebrated the following day. Candlemas was dedicated to new mothers and childbirth.

The start of summer was celebrated on 1 May, in the Celtic festival called Beltane. Given over to fertility and the reawakening of the earth, this was a free-for-all party, with singing, dancing, the lighting of more bonfires and a certain amount of licence. May Day continued the tradition in a diluted form. Dancing round the maypole, a pretty ritual, probably replaced a more ribald ceremony.

The charming custom of dancing round the maypole had its origin in a pagan fertility festival.
iStock

The last of the big four Celtic festivals took place on 1 August and was called Lughnasadh. This was the harvest festival, when the grain would be gathered in. The Christianised Saxons knew it as *hlaf-maesse*, meaning "loaf-mass", which later became corrupted to Lammas or Lammastide. The first loaves of bread made from the harvested grain were dedicated to God in a more general Festival of the First Fruits.

In between these four seasonal festivals were many others, some pagan and some of Christian origin, and others, like Easter and Christmas, a blend of the two. Lupercalia, the Roman celebration of youth, took place in the middle of February. In the warmer climes of the east it served as something of a harbinger of spring in which young people were encouraged to choose lovers. It had a reputation for excess that was thoroughly defused by the adoption in its place of the feast honouring the martyrdom of St Valentine, which took place on 14 February. Valentine was a gentleman committed to chastity, and it seems his association with romantic love was merely a matter of convenience. Nonetheless, St Valentine's Day remains one of the most popular traditions in the modern calendar, and people have been exchanging love tokens on this day for centuries.

Shrove Tuesday (Pancake Day, in modern parlance – the day before the first day of Lent, usually falling in mid-February) is the day when one of Derbyshire's greatest sporting spectacles takes place. The tradition of the Ashbourne Shrovetide football match was first documented in 1683, but it may be much older than that – and this is hardly football as the FA would recognise it!

The goals are two stone plinths at the sites of two old mills, Clifton and Sturston, three miles apart and separated by the Henmore Brook which flows through the town. At 2pm on Shrove Tuesday a special ball, made of leather and filled with cork, is "turned up", or launched into the air from a purpose-built platform in the centre of the town, which is the signal for the two teams ("Up'ards" and "Down'ards", depending on which side of the brook they are from) to start trying to get the ball, by pretty much any means other than transport by car, to the opposing team's goal.

This is mass football; there is no limit on the size of the teams, few rules (although one crucial one is that murder and manslaughter are prohibited), and the whole town is involved, as well as visitors who come from miles around to spectate or take part. Much of the action takes place in a giant scrum (known locally as the hug), and play can be frantic and rapid or slow and stagnant; indeed, sometimes the ball goes missing altogether. If neither team has won by 10pm the game continues on Ash Wednesday.

A Shrovetide football hug in the river – onlookers wait hopefully in case the ball appears.
iStock

Another, rather less violent Shrovetide custom is barring out, when school pupils would barricade their school against the master or mistress and try to prevent them from entering, often for a period of days. If they were successful they won the right to games or a holiday, but if the master managed to gain entry to the school he imposed extra lessons as punishment. This tradition was once widespread but had died out in most places by the turn of the century, but it persisted in Tideswell until the 1930s.

Finally on Shrove Tuesday, the ancient tradition of pancake racing is still practiced in Winster, having been revived as a fixture on the village calendar in the 1870s. The competition is fierce, with everyone from pre-schoolers to grandparents taking part in a series of races along the main street in the village – perhaps worth a visit if you prefer your sports a little less violent than the Ashbourne Football!

Although Easter honours the crucifixion and resurrection of Christ, there are many secular traditions attached to it which date from pre-Christian times. It is likely that the name Easter has been borrowed from a pagan goddess of the spring, Eostre. The Easter Bunny may well be a descendant of the hare, an animal associated with the spring and fertility and sacred to the Celts.

Eggs are a natural symbol of rebirth and were equally appropriate for both the Resurrection and for spring, the season in which Easter falls. It was once a common pastime on Easter Day for people to roll gaily coloured hard-boiled eggs down hillsides in a jovial race. This was called "pace-egging" or "egg-rolling", and it has been suggested that the rolling eggs represented the life-giving sun's passage through the sky, but it was also widely believed that if one's egg reached the bottom of the hill unscathed, good luck would surely follow.

"Lifting" was a widespread and peculiar custom, which was once carried out at Easter but has now died out. It took place on Easter Monday and Tuesday. A chair would be garlanded with flowers and people would take it in turns to sit in it while their fellows raised them into the air. It was common for men to lift women on Easter Monday and the other way round on Easter Tuesday, with the lifters claiming kisses and sometimes money as their rewards.

The archaic custom of lifting was popular on Easter Monday and the following Tuesday but has now completely died out.

A pleasant performance in the villages, it could be a rowdy affair in towns, where strangers were sometimes bundled into the chair and forced to pay a fee in order to be let down again. In all locations, however, the lifting ceased promptly at noon.

In parts of the Peak District Palm Sunday was known as Spanish Sunday, and was marked by a special drink made for and by children. The night before, a combination of Spanish liquorice, peppermint, lemon and sugar was put in a bottle and left to dissolve in a little water, and in the morning the resulting syrupy mixture was taken to the village well, diluted with pure spring water and shaken hard to mix, amid prayers and celebrations. In some locations, particularly the villages of Castleton and Bradwell in Derbyshire, this tradition occurred on Easter Sunday, with Palm Sunday being marked by a children's procession to the village well and the dropping of new pins into the waters – perhaps a folk memory of the ancient veneration of the spirits of place.

Other traditions relating to Easter are unarguably Christian, however. On Good Friday, the day of Christ's Crucifixion, we still eat hot cross buns. At one time it was common for all loaves to be marked with a cross. Despite its name, Good Friday's association made it an unlucky day in the minds of our ancestors. It has become a bank holiday because those engaged in dangerous occupations, such as mining and fishing, refused to work on that day. Blacksmiths and those in the building trades would often down tools too, because it was considered poor taste to handle nails on that day.

Easter itself was quite different in character. Easter Sunday was always given over to worship, while Easter Monday was a holiday for leisure and sports. Some believed that the sun danced on Easter Sunday in joyous memory of the resurrection, and it was formerly a custom to rise before dawn in the hope of seeing this phenomenon. It was also traditional to wear new clothes on Easter Sunday, or at least one item that had never been worn before.

Beating the bounds was another ritual commonly carried out at this time of the year, usually on Ascension Day (5 May). In the days before maps were freely available, it was important to clearly define parish boundaries and to ensure that nothing had occurred to alter them. Beating the bounds was sometimes taken rather too literally, however. The villagers, accompanied by a clergyman, would take the young boys of the parish on a tour of the landmarks on its boundary. At each one they would pause and the boys would be whipped to make sure they remembered them.

The ancient tradition of clipping (or clypping) the church was once widespread, but now takes place at only a few places across the country. One such is Wirksworth, where the local parishioners join hands to encircle the town's Church of St Mary and sing a special hymn, in an embrace (*clyppan*, in Anglo-Saxon) of the church and in celebration of its place at the heart of the community.

Clyppin, clyppan or clipping St Mary's Church in Wirksworth.
Image by Phil Richards

The day before the feast of St John the Baptist, or St John's Eve, falls on 23 June. It was also known as Midsummer Eve, even though the summer solstice – the longest day of the year – falls a couple of days before. Once again, this important stage in the year was celebrated with the lighting of bonfires. There were also numerous customs and celebrations associated with the bringing in of the harvest in the autumn, and traditional fairs and sales were held at Michaelmas, on 29 September.

The final great festival of the winter was, of course, Christmas. There is in fact no biblical reference to the date of Christ's birthday, and 25 December was chosen because it coincided with ancient pagan rituals associated with the winter solstice, the shortest day of the year, and with the birth dates of rival gods such as Mithras – 25 December became the Festival of the Unconquered Sun during the reign of the Roman Emperor Aurelius. It made sense for the early Christians to adopt a day already given over to celebration, especially one relating to the sense of hope engendered by the start of longer days and shorter nights.

Many of the old traditional customs associated with Christmas are of pre-Christian origin. Prince Albert, Queen Victoria's husband, is famously credited with bringing the custom of decorating a fir tree to Britain from his native Germany. In fact, there are records of an evergreen tree lit with candles being set up in a London street as long ago as the fifteenth century. This seems to have been a Norse tradition, as was the selecting of a Yule log, although the word "Yule" is Anglo-Saxon in origin.

The lighting of fires was a central element to the ancient Celtic celebrations. Fire gave warmth and light, allowed food to be cooked and represented that great life-bringer, the sun. Fire therefore brought luck and scared away the powers of darkness. The Yule log would be selected with great ceremony and celebration, in much the way we would choose a Christmas tree today. The larger the fireplace, the larger the log chosen to fill it. Lighting the log traditionally took place on Christmas Eve, ideally from a saved fragment from the previous year, and if it was big enough the log might bring warmth throughout Christmas Day and beyond.

Holly became associated with Christmas because it is an evergreen, and mistletoe simply because it was the plant most sacred to our Celtic ancestors. According to a Roman historian, the druids would only allow mistletoe to be cut with a golden sickle as it was so precious.

Cutting and bringing home the Yule log was a major occasion in big houses during the run up to Christmas.
iStock

The Twelve Days of Christmas, which included our present New Year's Day and Twelfth Night (6 January), were the perfect excuse for having a good time. Where possible, big family gatherings would be held or feasts where the servants as well as the masters would be entertained. Carols would be sung by the poor, and extra pennies collected to help them celebrate later on. A more boisterous variant on carol singing was the traditional wassailing. Wassail is an old English word meaning "be of good cheer". Poor people would walk round the parish singing wassailing songs either for money or, more usually, beer. Those who were better off might have in their possession a wassail cup, large and often of elaborate design, which they would fill with mulled beer or wine and use to toast each other. Mummers' plays – medieval morality plays – were also performed in many places.

In a custom dating back to Roman times, the roles of master and servant were overturned on one day of the year around Christmas time, with the staff served a feast by their employers. Sometimes a Lord of Misrule might be appointed from among the servants – a kind of fool king. In some military regiments even today the officers serve Christmas dinner to their men. Another custom was to lay the table for two on Christmas Eve, to welcome Joseph and Mary on Christmas morning. There was also a superstition that animals were able to talk on Christmas morning, and some people, particularly children, would creep to the pens and cowsheds as the sun rose in the hope of catching them doing so.

It was generally considered that using scissors on New Year's Day would bring bad fortune. However, the first water drawn from any pond, stream or well on New Year's Day was traditionally held to be lucky. It was known as the Flower of the Well, and there was often great competition to be the first to reach the water source after the stroke of midnight. If a young woman drew the water she would marry her true love within a twelve-month; if a farmer did so, he would often use it to wash his dairy utensils and then give it to his cattle to drink, to bless them for the year to come. Bottled and kept in a house, it would bring good luck to all who dwelled there.

Finally, it was also traditional to celebrate New Year's Day with a party, reflecting the universal belief that it is lucky to begin anything in good spirits. Of course, this tradition still holds true today.

> *I wish you a happy Christmas and a happy New Year,*
> *A pocket full of money and a cellar full of beer,*
> *And a good fat pig to last you all the year.*

Mistletoe, an unusual plant that is a parasite on other trees, is now closely associated with Christmas but at one time it was venerated by the Druids.

iStock

A PEAK DISTRICT MISCELLANY

The Peak District may have taken its name from the Pecsaetan, the "hill dwellers" who lived in the area during the Dark Ages, and not from its mainly flat-topped hills. The National Park was created in 1951, the first in the UK, to provide a protected playground for the inhabitants of the industrial cities of the north; it now attracts millions of visitors every year, who take advantage of its opportunities for walking, running, cycling, climbing, sailing, horse-riding and other outdoor pursuits of all descriptions. It is also known for its wildlife and its huge variety of habitats, providing for wide biodiversity and flora and fauna of all kinds.

Of course, no discussion of the Peak District would be complete without mentioning the world-famous Bakewell pudding (not to be confused with the much inferior Bakewell tart – make this mistake at your peril!). The true Derbyshire version of this dessert consists of a flaky pastry base, spread with jam, topped with an egg and almond custard and then baked until set.

There are several stories explaining the origin of the dish, and a number of shops in Bakewell claim to hold the original recipe – the most usual story is that it was first made by accident by a cook working at the Old White Horse Inn, which once occupied the site where the Rutland Arms now stands. Mrs Greaves, the landlady, left instructions for a kitchen maid to make a strawberry tart for a visiting nobleman, but instead of stirring the egg and almond mixture into the pastry, the girl spread it on top of the jam. The result was an immediate success, and a local legend was born.

There are several shops in Bakewell offering this teatime treat, each with their own jealously guarded secret recipe but all delicious. Eaten warm or cold, the genuine Bakewell pudding is a delicious and luxurious indulgence; you'll never go back to tarts again!

A true Bakewell pudding!
iStock

A more savoury local speciality is the oatcake, which is found in varying forms right across the Peak District. In general, the oatcake is a type of pancake made from oatmeal, flour, milk and yeast and cooked on a griddle. The Staffordshire version is smaller and thinner than its Derbyshire cousin, but both are usually served warm with fillings such as cheese, bacon, sausage or egg. They can also be eaten with sweet fillings such as jam or syrup, although this is generally frowned upon by purists. The Yorkshire or Lancashire (or Pennine) version is made without milk or flour, and may be dried and eaten as a cracker.

Finally in this Peak District miscellany – a mention of two sports unique to the region. The first, which was invented in the village of Wetton in Staffordshire in 1976, is Toe Wrestling. Competitors lock toes and try to force the other's foot to the ground – a lot like arm wrestling, but with toes. The World Championship now takes place at the Bentley Brook Inn at Fenny Bentley; Olympic inclusion was applied for, but was sadly turned down.

Meanwhile, every summer since the early 1990s the Barley Mow pub in the village of Bonsall has staged the World Hen Racing Championships. Competition is fierce, with highly trained chickens competing on a thirty-foot course over a series of elimination rounds. The track record is around three seconds, but races frequently take a lot longer (some birds even end up back at the start), and there is fierce rivalry between competing trainers. An event not to be missed!

Other Legends & Folklore books for you to enjoy

Legends & Folklore Cambridgeshire
ISBN 9781910551486

Legends & Folklore Cornwall
ISBN 9781912060696

Legends & Folklore Dorset
ISBN 9781910551493

Legends & Folklore Hampshire
ISBN 9781910551509

Legends & Folklore London
ISBN: 9781912060689

Legends & Folklore Nottinghamshire
ISBN 9781909914971

Legends & Folklore Scotland
ISBN 9781909914988

Legends & Folklore Somerset
ISBN 9781910551516

Legends & Folklore Wales
ISBN 9781909914995

Legends & Folklore Wiltshire
ISBN 9781910551004

Legends & Folklore Yorkshire
ISBN 9781912060719

Other Peak District books for you to enjoy

Bradwell's Images of Derbyshire Well Dressing
ISBN 9781912060658

Bradwell's Histories - Bess of Hardwick
ISBN 9781912060627

Walks for all Seasons Derbyshire
ISBN 9781912060528

Derbyshire Dialect
ISBN 9781902674483

Derbyshire Ghost Stories
ISBN 9781902674629

Derbyshire Murder Stories
ISBN 9781909914285

Derbyshire Recipes
ISBN 9781902674858

Derbyshire Wit & Humour
ISBN 9781909914513

Bradwell's Family Cycle Rides: The Peak District
ISBN 9781910551868

Bradwell's Images of the Peak District
ISBN 9781909914759

Bradwell's Longer Walks in the Peak District
ISBN 9781910551677

Bradwell's Pocket Walking Guides the Peak District
ISBN 9781910551936

Bradwells Book of The Peak District
ISBN 9781912060573

Colour the Peak District
ISBN 9781912060740

Walks for All Ages Peak District
ISBN 9781909914018